ADAPTED TO SURVIVE

ANIMALS THAT CLIMB

Angela Royston

Raintree is an imprint of Capstone Global Library Limited, a company incorporated in England and Wales having its registered office at 7 Pilgrim Street, London, EC4V 6LB – Registered company number: 6695582

www.raintreepublishers.co.uk
myorders@raintreepublishers.co.uk

Edited by Dan Nunn, Rebecca Rissman, and Helen Cox Cannons
Designed by Jo Hinton-Malivoire
Picture research by Mica Brancic
Production by Helen McCreath
Originated by Capstone Global Library Ltd
Printed and bound in China

ISBN 978 1 406 27085 3
17 16 15 14 13
10 9 8 7 6 5 4 3 2 1

British Library Cataloguing in Publication Data
A full catalogue record for this book is available from the British Library.

Acknowledgements
We would like to thank the following for permission to reproduce photographs: FLPA pp. 19 (Minden Pictures/Thomas Marent), 26 (Minden Pictures/Pete Oxford); Getty Images p. 18 (AFP Photo/Alfredo Estrella); Naturepl.com pp. 5 (© Eric Baccega), 6 (© Yukihiro Fukuda), 8 (© Kevin Schafer), 9 (ARCO/© Reinhard), 10, 24 (© Ingo Arndt), 11 (© Nature Production), 12 (2020VISION/© Peter Cairns), 14 (© Jouan & Rius), 15 (© Steven David Miller), 16 (© Andy Rouse), 17 (© Angela Scott), 23 (© Nick Garbutt); Science Photo Library p. 27 (Power and Syred); Shutterstock pp. 4 (© Redwood), 7 (© Irina Mos), 29 top left (© Foxtrot101), 29 bottom left (© Florence McGinn), 29 bottom right (© Eric Isselee), 29 top right (© Martin Lehmann); SuperStock pp. 13 (Prisma), 20 (Minden Pictures), 21 (Biosphoto), 22 (F1 ONLINE), 25 (age fotostock).

Cover photograph of a Victorian koala in a Eucalyptus tree, Adelaide, Australia, reproduced with permission of Shutterstock (© Cloudia Newland).

We would like to thank Michael Bright for his invaluable help in the preparation of this book.

Every effort has been made to contact copyright holders of material reproduced in this book. Any omissions will be rectified in subsequent printings if notice is given to the publisher.

Some words are shown in bold, **like this**. You can find out what they mean by looking in the glossary.

CONTENTS

GOOD AT CLIMBING

Many different types of animals are good at climbing. For example, squirrels climb up trees and poles and lizards scamper up steep rocks. Good climbers may be large or small.

Pandas are very good at climbing. But what makes them such good climbers?

CLIMBING TO SURVIVE

Climbing helps animals to **survive**. Being able to climb allows some animals to escape from danger and to find food in places other animals cannot reach.

A monkey can pick fruit from the top of a tree.

Bighorn sheep live high in the mountains. Their **hooves** grip the steep rocks and they move so fast they can usually escape from mountain lions, who hunt them.

ADAPTED TO CLIMB

Adaptations are special things about an animal's body that help it to **survive**. Animals have **adapted** to climbing in different ways. For example, many tree-climbers have sharp claws and strong legs.

three-toed sloth

two-toed sloth

DID YOU KNOW?
Sloths spend most of their lives hanging upside down in trees!

MOUNTAIN GOATS

Mountain goats are well **adapted** for living on steep mountainsides. They can spread and squeeze their **hooves**, so their rough **pads** are able to grip the smallest footholds. When a **predator** comes, the goats quickly find a safe ledge.

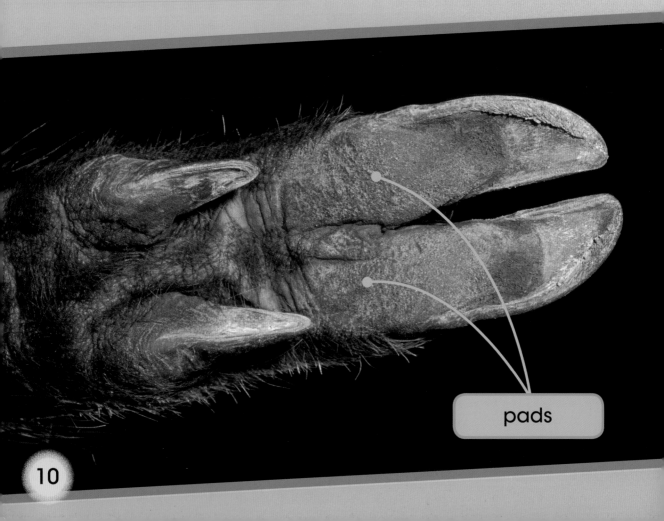

pads

Born climbers
Baby mountain goats begin to run and jump when they are just a few hours old.

SQUIRRELS

A squirrel is a champion tree climber.
It spreads its sharp claws to grip the
tree. Its bushy tail helps it to steer as
it jumps from tree to tree. Squirrels
are so light they can climb along the
thinnest branches to reach nuts to eat.

Squirrels cling on tightly
when a branch bends!

KOALAS

Koalas are well **adapted** to climbing trees. They have strong leg **muscles**, sharp claws, and rough **pads** on their paws to grip the bark. A koala is a **marsupial**. A marsupial mother carries her baby in her pouch.

Climbing kangaroo
Tree kangaroos are also marsupials that climb trees! They live high up in tropical forests.

LEOPARDS

Unlike most big cats, a leopard is at home in the trees. It grips the tree with its big feet and claws, and uses its long tail to balance. When a leopard kills an antelope, it eats some of it and hides the rest for later. Sometimes the leopard drags the **carcass** up a tree.

A leopard can sleep on the branch of a tree.

SPIDER MONKEYS

Spider monkeys live in South American rainforests. They have long arms and a long tail, which they use like an extra arm to grip the trees. A patch of bare skin at the end of their tail helps them to grip.

HANDY TAILS

A tail that can grip is called a **prehensile tail**. Spider monkeys are not the only animals that have them – chameleons and harvest mice have them, too. Harvest mice live in wheat fields and among tall grasses. They use their wide feet and long prehensile tail to help them climb from stalk to stalk.

chameleon

harvest mouse

TREE SNAKES

Tree snakes have long, thin bodies. They have no legs, so they grip the tree with their bodies. Tree snakes move easily from branch to branch. They also wind themselves around a branch to rest in the sunshine or wait for **prey**.

This green tree snake lives in forests in northern Australia.

Prehensile body
Tree snakes use their whole body like a **prehensile tail!**

GECKOS

A gecko lizard is an amazing climber. It has a **pad** at the end of each toe. The pad is covered with tiny, flat bristles that stick to most surfaces. A gecko can even walk across the ceiling to catch insects.

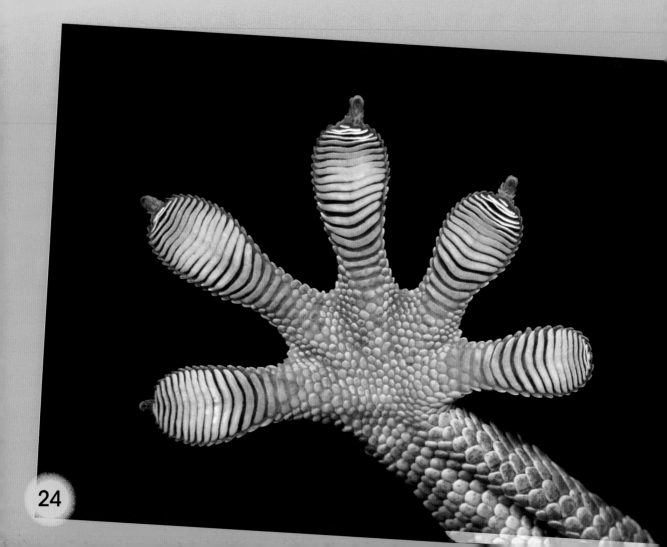

Smart move!
When the gecko wants to unstick its feet, it just curls up its toes!

TREE FROGS

A tree frog spends most of its life in trees. It hops from leaf to leaf on its long back legs. Each toe has a large, round **pad**. The pads are wet and stick to the leaves. They allow the frog to move safely.

A fly has hairy pads under its feet. The hairs make their own sticky glue!

hairy pads

ANIMAL CHALLENGE

1. Why can't a mountain goat climb tall trees?

2. What **adaptations** does a pet cat have to help it climb trees?

3. Which do you think can climb trees better – a gorilla or a dog?

Invent a new climbing animal! Think about where your animal will climb and why. You can use some of the adaptations shown in the photos, or make up your own.

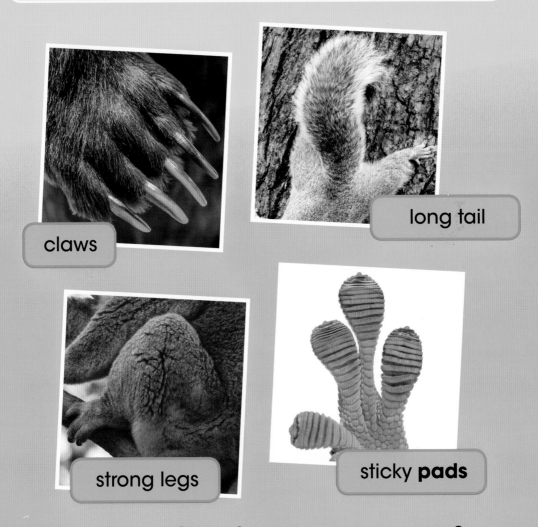

claws

long tail

strong legs

sticky **pads**

GLOSSARY

adaptation special thing about an animal's body that helps it to survive in a particular way or in a particular habitat

adapted well suited to a particular activity or way of living

carcass dead body of an animal

hooves hard covers that protect the feet of some animals, such as goats and horses

marsupial animal that carries its newborn baby in a pouch on the mother's body

muscle fleshy part of the body that makes a particular part of the body move

pad soft, tough cushion under the feet of many animals

predator animal that hunts and kills other animals for food

prehensile tail tail that is able to grip or hold onto something

prey animal that is hunted and eaten by another animal

survive manage to go on living

FIND OUT MORE

BOOKS

Animal (Dorling Kindersley, 2011)

Animal Encyclopedia (Dorling Kindersley, 2008)

WEBSITES

kids.nationalgeographic.co.uk/kids/animals/creaturefeature
Click on particular animals, such as sloths or geckos, to find out more about them.

www.bbc.co.uk/nature/adaptations/Climbing
This BBC website gives several short videos of animals that climb to survive, including mountain goats, spider monkeys, and tree kangaroos.

www.ypte.org.uk/animal-facts.php
Find out more about many different animals on this website.

INDEX